C000145376

I, CLAUDIO

I, CLAUDIO

THE WIT AND
WISDOM OF RANIERI

BLINK
bringing you closer

Published by Blink Publishing
3.25, The Plaza,
535 Kings Road,
Chelsea Harbour,
London, SW10 0SZ

www.blinkpublishing.co.uk

facebook.com/blinkpublishing
twitter.com/blinkpublishing

HB – 9781911274391
Ebook – 9781911274407

A CIP catalogue of this book is available from the British Library.

Typeset by www.envydesignltd.co.uk

Printed and bound by Clays Ltd, St Ives Plc

1 3 5 7 9 10 8 6 4 2

Blink Publishing is an imprint of the Bonnier Publishing Group
www.bonnierpublishing.co.uk

CONTENTS

THE NAYSAYERS

CLAUDIO RANIERI? REALLY?

GARY LINEKER ON TWITTER, 13TH JULY 2015

THEY SHOULD REALLY HAVE SIGNED HIS AGENT. HE GOT ALL THOSE JOBS FOR HIM! I MAY BE QUITE WRONG, BUT I DON'T THINK HE'S EVER WON ANYTHING.

SKY SPORTS PUNDIT AND FORMER ENGLAND DEFENDER
PHIL THOMPSON, 13TH JULY 2015

RANIERI, GOOD MANAGER BUT FOR ME NOT LEICESTER. IF YOU PLAY FOR THE FOXES YOU NEED SOMEONE YOU CAN RELATE TO AS A MANAGER... BIG NAME, BAD CHOICE IN MY OPINION! TIME WILL TELL! HOPEFULLY I'M WRONG!

ROBBIE SAVAGE ON TWITTER, 13TH JULY 2015

I'M ASTONISHED. I JUST DIDN'T SEE THIS ONE COMING. OBVIOUSLY THERE HAVE BEEN MANY PEOPLE LINKED TO THE JOB BUT AS FAR AS I'M AWARE, RANIERI WASN'T ONE AND FOR ME, IT IS A STRANGE APPOINTMENT.

SKY SPORTS PUNDIT AND FORMER LEICESTER STRIKER
TONY COTTEE, 13TH JULY 2015

RANIERI IS A NICE GUY, BUT HE'S DONE WELL TO GET THE LEICESTER JOB. AFTER WHAT HAPPENED WITH GREECE, AM SURPRISED HE CAN WALK BACK INTO PL.

HARRY REDKNAPP ON TWITTER, 13TH JULY 2015

CAN'T BELIEVE LEICESTER APPOINTED RANIERI... GREAT CLUB, GREAT FANBASE BUT I'M AFRAID MK RATHER THAN OLD TRAFFORD SEASON AFTER NEXT.

DIETMAR HAMANN ON TWITTER, 13TH JULY 2015

I'M NOT CONVINCED ABOUT 'TINKERMAN' CLAUDIO RANIERI. PEARSON HAD THE DRESSING ROOM. THE PLAYERS BELIEVED IN HIM. RANIERI HAS A JOB ON HIS HANDS EARNING THE SAME RESPECT.

STAN COLLYMORE, 7TH AUGUST 2015

REPLACING NIGEL PEARSON WITH CLAUDIO RANIERI CAN ONLY BE DESCRIBED AS A HUGE PUNT. THE RISK IS THAT CITY NOW LOSE SOME OF THE ENERGY, AGGRESSION AND SPIRIT THAT PULLED THEM TO SAFETY.

*SKY SPORTS COMMENTATOR AND FORMER LEICESTER STRIKER
ALAN SMITH, 3RD AUGUST 2015*

WITH LEICESTER I THINK IT COULD BE A MASSIVE STRUGGLE THIS SEASON. I THINK HE MIGHT STRUGGLE WITH THE SPIRIT THERE.

MATT LE TISSIER, JULY 2015

IF LEICESTER WANTED SOMEONE NICE, THEY'VE GOT HIM. IF THEY WANTED SOMEONE TO KEEP THEM IN THE PREMIER LEAGUE, THEN THEY MAY HAVE GONE FOR THE WRONG GUY.

THE GUARDIAN *WRITER MARCUS CHRISTENSON, 14TH JULY 2015*

FOLLOWING TODAY'S DEVASTATING RESULT FOR THE NATIONAL TEAM, I TAKE FULL RESPONSIBILITY FOR THE MOST UNFORTUNATE CHOICE OF COACH, WHICH HAS RESULTED IN SUCH A POOR IMAGE OF THE NATIONAL TEAM BEING PUT BEFORE THE FANS.

GEORGIOS SARRIS, PRESIDENT OF THE HELLENIC FOOTBALL FEDERATION, 15TH NOVEMBER 2014, FOLLOWING RANIERI'S GREECE SIDE'S DEFEAT TO THE FAROE ISLANDS.

CLAUDIO RANIERI IS CLEARLY EXPERIENCED, BUT THIS IS AN UNINSPIRED CHOICE BY LEICESTER.

GARY LINEKER, 13TH JULY 2015

TO SAY HE IS HIT AND MISS IS AN UNDERSTATEMENT. HE IS MAINLY MISS...

PUNDIT AND FORMER LEICESTER STRIKER
STEVE CLARIDGE, 15TH JULY 2015

ARE THERE SERIOUSLY NO MANAGERS AROUND THAT WE HAVE TO BE ROLLING OUT RANIERI AGAIN IN THE PREMIER LEAGUE?

KICK IT OUT DEVELOPMENT MANAGER
TROY TOWNSEND, 13TH JULY 2015

I'M NOT SURE WHAT'S WORSE – NEWC APPTING JOE KINNEAR OR LEICS RANIERI. HE'LL BE ONE OF THE FIRST 3 SACKED THIS SEASON.

PRESENTER RICHARD KEYS ON TWITTER,
13TH JULY 2015

HE IS ALMOST 70, AND HE HAS WON A SUPER CUP AND ANOTHER SMALL CUP. HE'S TOO OLD TO CHANGE MENTALITY. HE'S OLD AND HE HASN'T WON ANYTHING.

JOSÉ MOURINHO, 8TH OCTOBER 2015

ON HIS CRITICS
AND RIVALS

I DON'T BELIEVE THE BOOKMAKERS. AT THE BEGINNING OF THE SEASON THE BOOKMAKERS SAID, 'SACK RANIERI'. I HOPE ONE TIME THEY ARE RIGHT!

RESPONDING TO THE NEWS THAT HE HAD BEEN THE BOOKIES' FAVOURITE FOR THE FIRST PREMIER LEAGUE MANAGERIAL SACKING, FEBRUARY 2016

NO, I WILL BE SACKED IN MAY!

*RESPONDING TO CHARLTON FANS' TAUNTS OF
'YOU'RE BEING SACKED IN THE SUMMER' IN MARCH 2004*

I AM NOT LIKE MOURINHO, I DON'T HAVE TO WIN THINGS TO BE SURE OF MYSELF.

AFTER HIS JUVENTUS SIDE SUFFERED A 3–0 DEFEAT TO HAMBURG IN THE 2008 EMIRATES CUP

BEFORE I WAS 'THE TINKERMAN' AND NOW IT'S TOO MUCH THE SAME!

REACTING TO CRITICISM ABOUT NOT ROTATING HIS PLAYERS, NOVEMBER 2015

DO I COME HERE WITH SOMETHING TO PROVE? I LOVE MY JOB. I WANT TO IMPROVE ALL MY PLAYERS, I WANT TO IMPROVE EVERYTHING. THE GAMES, THE POINTS WE ACHIEVE ARE IMPORTANT. OTHER THINGS ARE NOT IMPORTANT.

IN RESPONSE TO CRITICISM ABOUT HIS APPOINTMENT, JULY 2015

AM I DISAPPOINTED WITH THE REACTION? YES. I UNDERSTAND BUT I WILL WORK HARD TO MAKE CHANGES. I RESPECT EVERYBODY. BUT NOW MY PROBLEM IS NOT LINEKER OR REDKNAPP OR MARK BOSNICH. MY FOCUS IS ON LEICESTER.

ON CRITICISM ABOUT HIS APPOINTMENT, 21ST JULY 2015

AT VALENCIA, I WON THE COPA DEL REY FOR THE FIRST TIME IN 25 YEARS. I CAN STOP OR SHALL I CONTINUE? ALSO IN GREECE I WANTED TO BUILD SOMETHING BUT IT'S DIFFICULT TO BUILD ON THE SAND.

IN RESPONSE TO CRITICISM ABOUT HIS APPOINTMENT, JULY 2015

IT WAS MY FAULT. AFTER 30 YEARS IN FOOTBALL I KNOW I HAVE TO ACCEPT THAT. WITH ONE PLAYER MORE I WANTED TO WIN THE MATCH. EVERYBODY WANTED TO DO SOMETHING MORE, TO RUN WITH BALL AND NOT TO COMBINE WITH THE OTHER PLAYERS.

AFTER LOSING THE CHAMPIONS LEAGUE SEMI-FINAL IN APRIL 2004 TO MONACO

I MADE A MISTAKE WHEN I WAS MANAGER OF GREECE. I HAD FOUR MATCHES AND FOR EACH GAME I TRAINED THE PLAYERS FOR JUST THREE DAYS. THAT IS 12 DAYS OF TRAINING. WHAT CAN I DO IN JUST 12 DAYS? I HAD TO REBUILD A NATIONAL TEAM IN JUST 12 DAYS. WHAT COULD I DO? I AM NOT A MAGICIAN.

REFLECTING ON HIS DISASTROUS STINT AS MANAGER OF GREECE, MAY 2016

BUT YOU KNOW, SOMETHING STRANGE ARRIVED AND THEY SACKED ME. AND I SAID: 'THIS IS NOT MY JOB, I LOVE THE PITCH, I LOVE FOOTBALL BUT THERE IS SO MUCH POLITICS AND I AM NOT A POLITICS MAN. I'M A CLEAR MAN.' SO I SAID: 'IT'S NOT MY JOB.'

ON HIS SACKING FROM SERIE C TEAM PUTEOLANA, MAY 2016

BEFORE YOU KILL ME, YOU CALL ME THE 'DEAD MAN WALKING'. I MUST BUY YOU AN ESPRESSO. BUT ONLY A LITTLE ONE – I AM SCOTTISH!

ON HIS IMMINENT DEPARTURE FROM CHELSEA, JUNE 2004

HELLO MY SHARKS, WELCOME TO THE FUNERAL.

AT A PRESS CONFERENCE SHORTLY BEFORE CHELSEA WERE KNOCKED OUT OF THE CHAMPIONS LEAGUE BY MONACO IN 2004

I THINK EVERYONE NOW ROTATES. THE TINKERMAN WAS ONE, NOW THERE ARE A LOT OF TINKERMEN!

MUSING ON HIS FORMER NICKNAME, JULY 2015

YES, BIG REVENGE... I WANT TO KILL HIM! HE'S A NICE MAN. IT'S JUST FOOTBALL.

*BEFORE FACING WATFORD BOSS QUIQUE SANCHEZ FLORES,
WHO REPLACED HIM AT VALENCIA, 9TH NOVEMBER 2015*

AN IDIOT DOESN'T BECOME EINSTEIN OVERNIGHT OR EVEN IN THE SPACE OF 15 DAYS. IT'S THE SAME MAN WORKING HERE. I MADE MISTAKES BEFORE AND I WILL MAKE THEM AGAIN, THE DIFFERENCE IS THAT IN THE PAST I LOST AND NOW I'M WINNING.

WHILE MANAGING JUVENTUS FOLLOWING AN UPTURN IN RESULTS IN 2011

I, CLAUDIO

I AM A LOVELY MAN AS LONG AS EVERYONE DOES WHAT I SAY.

ON BECOMING CHELSEA MANAGER, 2000

ROBERT DE NIRO WOULD BE GOOD. I'VE HEARD THAT'S WHO THEY WANT TO PLAY ME.

WHEN ASKED WHO WOULD PLAY THE LEICESTER CITY BOSS IN A
POTENTIAL FILM ABOUT THE CLUB, APRIL 2016

WHEN I LOSE THE PASSION I WILL STOP, BUT I DON'T KNOW IF I COULD EVER LOSE THE PASSION.

*WHEN ASKED IF HE WOULD EVER LOSE HIS DESIRE
TO BE A MANAGER, 2ND OCTOBER 2015*

I WILL KEEP IT IN MY HOME AND WHEN THERE IS A BAD MOMENT I WILL TAKE IT OUT, LOOK AT IT AND SAY, 'HEH, COME ON MAN – BALANCE.'

TALKING ABOUT HIS PREMIER LEAGUE WINNER'S MEDAL

I'M A PRAGMATIC MAN – I JUST WANTED TO WIN MATCH AFTER MATCH. NEVER DID I THINK TOO MUCH ABOUT WHERE IT WOULD TAKE US.

SHORTLY AFTER WINNING THE PREMIER LEAGUE, MAY 2016

I AM A CALM PERSON, EVEN WHEN I WAS YOUNG. I HAVEN'T BEEN IN A DISCO MORE THAN 10 TIMES.

MAINTAINING HIS COMPOSURE ON THE FINAL DAY OF THE SEASON, MAY 2016

I CAN'T CHANGE NOW. I'M LIKE FRANK SINATRA – I ALWAYS DO IT MY WAY. I TOLD THE PLAYERS EVERYTHING I DID IN THE MONACO GAME WAS WRONG. I CHANGED THINGS TO WIN THE MATCH – BUT WE LOST AND I WAS THINKING, 'OH F***, CLAUDIO, WHY, WHY? BAD TINKERMAN!'

ON HIS DISASTROUS ATTACKING SUBSTITUTIONS DURING THE CHAMPIONS LEAGUE SEMI-FINAL FIRST LEG AFTER MONACO HAD A MAN SENT OFF. CHELSEA LOST 3–1. APRIL 2004.

WATCHING CHELSEA ON MONDAY I WAS AT FIRST ON THE ARMCHAIR BUT AFTER [THE HAZARD GOAL] ON THE CEILING!

AN EXCITABLE TINKERMAN AFTER EDEN HAZARD EQUALIZED AGAINST SPURS, SECURING THE PREMIER LEAGUE CROWN FOR LEICESTER, 4TH MAY 2016

I'M CONCENTRATING TO BE CALM, BUT OF COURSE I'M VERY, VERY HAPPY INSIDE. MY BLOOD IS UNBELIEVABLE.

TRYING TO CONTAIN HIS EMOTIONS AFTER WINNING THE PREMIER LEAGUE, 7TH MAY 2016

I WANT TO BE THE MOST CRAZY MAN AND TEAM IN THE PREMIER LEAGUE.

ON LEICESTER HOLDING TOP SPOT IN THE PREMIER LEAGUE IN THE MIDDLE OF JANUARY 2016

IT'S FANTASTIC WHEN YOU SEE BEFORE THE MATCH, AN OLD LADY WITH A LEICESTER SHIRT OUTSIDE THE STADIUM. I SAY: 'UNBELIEVABLE. THEY COME FROM LEICESTER TO SUPPORT US.' THIS IS MY EMOTION.

AN EMOTIONAL CLAUDIO THANKS LEICESTER FANS FOR HELPING THEM TO WITHIN THREE WINS OF THE TITLE, APRIL 2016

I AM USED TO WORKING WITH MY FRIEND PRESSURE. FORTUNATELY I HAVE ALREADY GONE GREY FROM MY OTHER CHAIRMEN.

CLAUDIO: COOL, CALM, COLLECTED, MARCH 2004

YOU TELL THEM CLAUDIO EVEN
ROTATES THE BOOKS!

AFTER CLAUDIO ADMITTED TO A JOURNALIST TO HAVING THREE BOOKS
ON THE GO SIMULTANEOUSLY, APRIL 2016

I DON'T KNOW ENGLISH THAT WELL. I CAN HEAR THEM SAYING 'RANIERI' AND SOMETHING ELSE. I HOPE THEY'RE PRAISING ME!

EVER THE OPTIMIST, APRIL 2016

ON PLAYERS

I SCOUTED CRISTIANO RONALDO – NOT A BAD YOUNG PLAYER!

RANIERI REVEALS WHAT HE GOT UP TO DURING A BREAK TO ROME IN FEBRUARY 2016

NO-ONE CAN BUY VARDY OR MAHREZ IN JANUARY. THEY DON'T HAVE THE MONEY AND THEY DON'T HAVE A PRICE.

STEERING ANY WOULD-BE SUITORS AWAY FROM HIS PRIZE ASSETS, DECEMBER 2015

THIS PLAYER – HE WAS RUNNING SO HARD I THOUGHT HE MUST HAVE A PACK FULL OF BATTERIES HIDDEN IN HIS SHORTS.

ON LEICESTER MIDFIELDER N'GOLO KANTE'S SEEMINGLY ENDLESS RESERVES OF ENERGY, APRIL 2016

I GAVE THE PLAYERS SOME PROGRAMMES AND THEY RESPECTED IT AND WORKED WELL. WE HAD THEIR GPS AND WHEN THEY CAME BACK THE RESULTS WERE GOOD.

AFTER GIVING THE PLAYERS A WEEK OFF, BUT ALSO ISSUING THEM WITH STRICT FITNESS INSTRUCTIONS, FEBRUARY 2016

TOMORROW, TRAINING SESSION. BAD LADS!

AFTER BEING SOAKED WITH CHAMPAGNE BY CHRISTIAN FUCHS
ON THE FINAL DAY OF THE SEASON, MAY 2016

COME ON JAMIE, WE NEED YOU! I NEED YOU!

WHAT CLAUDIO TOLD JAMIE VARDY AFTER A GOALLESS FIRST HALF
AGAINST SUNDERLAND. HE SCORED TWICE AND LEICESTER WON 2–0, APRIL 2016

MAKELELE IS THE CONDUCTOR OF MY ORCHESTRA – HE IS THE BATTERY IN THE ENGINE.

ON HIS DEFENSIVE MIDFIELD DYNAMO, SEPTEMBER 2003

DENNIS WISE IS A VERY INTELLIGENT PERSON. AND ALTHOUGH I DO NOT SPEAK ENGLISH, YOU CAN SPEAK TO HIM WITH YOUR EYES.

CHANNELLING HIS INNER HYPNOTIST, SEPTEMBER 2000

IF RIYAD [MAHREZ] IS OUR LIGHT, JAMIE [VARDY] IS OUR AEROPLANE, OUR RAF. IT IS IMPORTANT TO HAVE A GOALSCORER BECAUSE OTHERWISE YOU NEVER SCORE A GOAL.

*CLAUDIO'S UNIQUE BLEND OF METAPHOR
AND TRUISM, MAY 2016*

HE IS A GREAT YOUNGSTER WITH A GREAT FUTURE BUT HE MUST CHANGE HIS MENTALITY. SOMETIMES THE FRENCH MENTALITY IS, TODAY I PLAY WELL, MAYBE I'LL PLAY WELL TOMORROW.

CLAUDIO'S THOUGHTS ABOUT ANTHONY MARTIAL, SEPTEMBER 2015

TWO YEARS AGO I WATCHED CARLTON PLAY FOR THE RESERVES AND I SAW TWO ANIMALS IN HIM – ONE WAS A RABBIT AND THE OTHER A LION. I WANT TO SEE THAT LION COME OUT IN HIM MORE OFTEN.

ON THE MISFIRING STRIKER CARLTON COLE, 2004

I ONCE SAID JIMMY FLOYD HASSELBAINK IS
LIKE A SHARK AND CARLTON COLE LIKE A
LION. WELL, ADRIAN MUTU IS ANOTHER BORN
PREDATOR. IN FACT, MUTU IS LIKE A SNAKE.

A BORN NATURALIST, AUGUST 2003

HE IS MY NEW LITTLE LION.
AND I LIKE LIONS.

ANIMAL LOVER CLAUDIO ON HERNAN CRESPO, THE NEW ADDITION
TO HIS PRIDE, SEPTEMBER 2003

THIS IS NOT A FOOTBALLER.
THIS IS A FANTASTIC HORSE.

DESCRIBING SUPERSTAR STRIKER JAMIE VARDY, APRIL 2016

ONE DAY, I'M GOING TO SEE YOU CROSS THE BALL, AND THEN FINISH THE CROSS WITH A HEADER YOURSELF.

CLAUDIO ON MIDFIELD DYNAMO N'GOLO KANTE, APRIL 2016

LITTLE GIANFRANCO ZOLA HAS IN THE BOOT THE REMOTE CONTROL.

ON HIS FAVOURITE ITALIAN'S TECHNICAL WIZARDRY, MAY 2003

JOHN TERRY, YOU KNOW, HE WAS LIKE MY SON. I BELIEVED IN HIM WHEN HE WAS YOUNG.

ON HIS STRONG BOND WITH THE CHELSEA STALWART DEFENDER, MAY 2016

JOHN IS AN EXTRA-TERRESTRIAL – I THINK HE'S FROM MARS. HE'S LIKE ET AND NEEDS TO PHONE HOME!

ON JOHN TERRY'S OTHERWORLDLY TALENTS, MARCH 2003

THE
THINKERMAN

IF IT IS THE CASE THAT YOU NEED JUST A FIRST 11 AND THREE OR FOUR MORE PLAYERS, THEN WHY DID CHRISTOPHER COLUMBUS SAIL TO INDIA TO DISCOVER AMERICA?

CLAUDIO'S UNIQUE APPROACH TO ASSEMBLING HIS SQUAD, APRIL 2004

ONE DAY MAYBE, WHEN I'VE GONE OR I AM WAVING GOODBYE TO THIS EARTH, BUT NOT NOW. IN ITALY WE SAY IF YOU GET A MONUMENT IT'S BECAUSE YOU'RE DEAD. SO, JUST WAIT TO MAKE THE MONUMENT.

ON CALLS TO ERECT A STATUE IN LEICESTER IN HIS HONOUR, APRIL 2016

FOR ME IT'S NOT IMPORTANT WHAT A MANAGER IS DOING IN A LITTLE PERIOD, IT'S ABOUT THE BIG PERIOD.

*CLAUDIO'S THOUGHTS ON HIS SACKING FROM THE
GREECE NATIONAL TEAM, DECEMBER 2015*

...HE JUST STOOD THERE FOR A WEEK WATCHING US AND HAS HARDLY SAID ANYTHING.

LEICESTER CITY LEGEND ALAN BIRCHENALL RECALLS ASKING ONE OF LEICESTER'S PLAYERS ABOUT CLAUDIO'S FIRST FEW DAYS AT THE CLUB, APRIL 2016

THERE IS A GOOD QUOTE FROM KIPLING. WHEN HE SAID 'VICTORY AND DEFEAT, IT'S THE SAME.' IT'S NOT GOOD OR BAD. YOU HAVE TO STAY IN THE MIDDLE.

BENEATH CLAUDIO'S EXCITABLE EXTERIOR LIES THE INNER FOCUS OF A ZEN MASTER, DECEMBER 2015

THE THINKERMAN

*WHEN ASKED WHAT HIS NEW NICKNAME SHOULD BE AFTER LEADING
LEICESTER TO THE PREMIER LEAGUE TITLE, MAY 2016*

LIFE IS FULL OF OPPORTUNITY, IT'S IMPORTANT TO TAKE THE RIGHT OPPORTUNITY.

MAY 2016

THE FOOD, WEATHER AND THE WOMEN ARE NICE.

WHEN ASKED WHAT HE LIKED ABOUT MONACO

IT IS CRAZY. IT IS A CRAZY PREMIER LEAGUE.

ON HIS TEAM HOLDING THE TOP SPOT IN THE LEAGUE, FEBRUARY 2016

I HAVE READ ABOUT WHO IS TOP AT CHRISTMAS DAY WILL WIN THE LEAGUE, BLAH, BLAH, BLAH... BUT THIS IS A STRANGE LEAGUE. EVERYTHING IS STRANGE.

CLAUDIO NOT GETTING AHEAD OF HIMSELF, DECEMBER 2015

ALL THE PEOPLE AROUND THE WORLD ARE ASKING FOR LEICESTER, WHAT HAPPENED, AND THIS IS A MOMENT YOU HAVE TO LEAVE FOR A LITTLE MORE TIME AND TASTE SLOWLY, LIKE A GOOD WINE. SAVOUR IT.

ON ENJOYING THE MOMENT FOR AS LONG AS POSSIBLE, MAY 2016

PICASSO. YES. STRANGE, BUT OKAY. MY WIFE IS THE EXPERT, BUT I LIKE ART PARTICULARLY. I LIKE VAN GOGH.

REVEALING HIS ARTISTIC SENSIBILITIES, APRIL 2002

OUR PITCH IS GOOD... FOR CARROTS AND POTATOES.

CLAUDIO'S THOUGHTS ON THE STATE OF THE STAMFORD BRIDGE PITCH, 2003

IN ITALY THE COACH IS A PARATROOPER WHO JUMPS OUT OF THE PLANE BUT DOESN'T KNOW IF THE PARACHUTE WILL OPEN OR NOT.

ON THE PERILS OF MANAGING IN SERIE A, 2004

FOOTBALL MANAGERS ARE LIKE A PARACHUTIST. AT TIMES IT DOESN'T OPEN. HERE, IT IS AN UMBRELLA. YOU UNDERSTAND, MARY POPPINS?

SOMETHING IS LOST IN TRANSLATION SHORTLY AFTER CLAUDIO ARRIVES AT CHELSEA, 2000

THE
TINKERMAN'S
TACTICS

I DON'T ASK OF YOU THAT YOU WIN, BUT THAT YOU ALWAYS GIVE EVERYTHING YOU'VE GOT.

ON HOW WINNING ISN'T EVERYTHING, MAY 2016

I TOLD MY PLAYERS I WANTED THEM TO PLAY ENGLISH FOOTBALL AND I PUT MY LITTLE ITALIAN TACTICS WITH THEIR ENGLISH HEART AND THEN WE CAN DO SOMETHING SPECIAL.

ON CLAUDIO'S MAGIC MANAGERIAL FORMULA, MAY 2016

I WILL KILL THEM WITH MY BARE HANDS, I WILL THROTTLE THEM!

CLAUDIO'S WARNING IF HIS TEAM WEREN'T FULLY PREPARED FOR THEIR CLASH WITH EVERTON ON 7TH MAY 2016

FROM THE BEGINNING, WHEN SOMETHING WAS WRONG, I SAID 'DILLY-DING, DILLY-DONG, WAKE UP' DURING TRAINING SESSIONS. AND ON CHRISTMAS DAY I BOUGHT FOR EACH OF THE PLAYERS A LITTLE BELL, JUST AS A JOKE. IT WAS A FUNNY THING.

THE ECCENTRIC HABITS OF SANTA CLAUDIO, MARCH 2016

MY TEAM IS LIKE AN ORCHESTRA. TO PLAY THE SYMPHONY CORRECTLY I NEED SOME OF THE BOOM-BOOM BUT ALSO SOME OF THE TWEET-TWEET. SOMETIMES THE BOOM AND THE TWEET GO WELL TOGETHER.

CLAUDIO THE CONDUCTOR, APRIL 2004

IT'S IMPORTANT NOT TO LOOK DOWN OR BEHIND YOU. LIKE A CLIMBER, YOU NEED TO LOOK UP. IF YOU LOOK DOWN, YOU GO, 'OH! MY GOD, LOOK WHERE WE ARE!'

ON ENCOURAGING HIS PLAYERS TO STAY FOCUSED, FEBRUARY 2016

WHEN I TALK TO THE PLAYERS I SPEAK FIRST OF ALL IN ENGLISH, THEN I SAY, 'SORRY, NOW I WILL SPEAK IN SPANISH, OR ITALIAN'. THEN ON THE TOUCHLINE I SPEAK ANOTHER LANGUAGE SO THE OTHER MANAGER DOESN'T UNDERSTAND WHAT I AM SAYING!

CLAUDIO REFLECTING ON USING THE LANGUAGE BARRIER TO HIS ADVANTAGE, SEPTEMBER 2003

I ALWAYS TELL MY PLAYERS TO FIND THE FIRE WITHIN THEMSELVES. A CHANCE LIKE THIS WILL NEVER COME ROUND AGAIN. SEEK THAT FIRE, DON'T BE ASHAMED OF IT.

RED-HOT ADVICE FROM THE GAFFER, FEBRUARY 2016

I ALWAYS TELL HIM TO SHOOT AT GOAL BECAUSE IF YOU DON'T SHOOT YOU CAN'T SCORE A GOAL.

BACK-TO-BASICS ADVICE FOR DANNY DRINKWATER

I TOLD MY PLAYERS, 'WHEN YOU GO ON THE PITCH AND YOU HEAR THE SONG FROM KASABIAN, THAT MEANS THEY WANT WARRIORS'. I WANT TO SEE THEM AS WARRIORS FOR THE FANS.

ON HOW HEARING 'FIRE' BY KASABIAN HELPED SPUR HIS TEAM TO VICTORY AGAINST SUNDERLAND ON THE FIRST DAY OF THE SEASON

I WAS LIKE PAVAROTTI OUT THERE, TRYING TO STIMULATE MY PLAYERS.

ON HIS ANIMATED SHOUTING FROM THE TOUCHLINE, 2004

WHEN I GOT HERE, ONE COACH WAS TRAINING A PLAYER'S HAIR, AND ANOTHER WAS TRAINING ANOTHER PART OF HIS BODY.

HERE'S HOPING SOMETHING GOT LOST IN TRANSLATION... MARCH 2001

MY PLAYERS, MYSELF, EVERYBODY AT THE TRAINING GROUND COMES TO OUR JOB WITH A SMILE – THAT IS MY PHILOSOPHY. I DON'T WANT TO SEE SAD PEOPLE AROUND ME. LIFE IS HARD AND IT IS IMPORTANT TO STAY TOGETHER SMILING.

ON HIS SPECIAL BRAND OF BONHOMIE, MARCH 2016

I WOULD LOVE TO BE ABLE TO STICK MY PLAYERS IN A FREEZER WHEN THEY COME OFF THE PITCH AT THE END OF THE GAME – AND THEN TAKE THEM OUT AGAIN JUST BEFORE THE NEXT ONE.

CLAUDIO'S CRYOGENIC STRATEGY, SEPTEMBER 2002

BE SMART – YOU ARE FOXES.

*ACCORDING TO WINGER RIYAD MAHREZ, CLAUDIO ALWAYS SAYS
THESE FIVE WORDS BEFORE EACH MATCH*

THE DAY MY PLAYERS RELAX I GET CRAZY. THEY KNOW THAT. I THINK I AM A NICE MAN BUT ALSO I AM DEMANDING, THAT IS OUR WAY.

ON HIS DEMAND FOR INTENSITY, DECEMBER 2015

ON THE
IMPOSSIBLE
DREAM

WHY CAN'T WE CONTINUE TO RUN, RUN, RUN? WE ARE LIKE FORREST GUMP. LEICESTER IS FORREST GUMP. I GIVE YOU THE HEADLINE THERE.

ON HOW HIS PLAYERS COULD GO THE DISTANCE, DECEMBER 2015

WE KNOW VERY WELL NEXT SEASON EVERYTHING WILL BE DIFFERENT BUT THE FANS ARE DREAMING – KEEP DREAMING. WHY WAKE UP?

*A JUBILANT CLAUDIO AT THE PRESS CONFERENCE ON THE
FINAL DAY OF THE SEASON, MAY 2016*

I'VE ENJOYED TODAY WITH OUR FANS. I WANT TO SAY THANK YOU TO OUR FANS, THEY BELIEVED IN US EVEN WHEN WE WERE 2-0 DOWN IN GAMES, THEY PUSHED US. THE TEAM PLAYED WITH ITS HEART AND SOUL AND THE PEOPLE SAW THIS.

CLAUDIO ADDRESSING THE CROWD AT LEICESTER'S TITLE CELEBRATIONS, MAY 2016

IT IS IMPORTANT TO FINISH THE STORY LIKE AN AMERICAN MOVIE. ALWAYS IN THE END IT IS OK. THERE IS A HAPPY ENDING.

ENCOURAGING HIS PLAYERS TO FINISH THE SEASON WITH A FLOURISH, APRIL 2016

IT WILL BE A VERY GOOD ATMOSPHERE WITH THE MUSIC. I HOPE WE ARE READY, NOT JUST TO LISTEN TO THE MUSIC BUT TO DO SOME MUSIC.

THINKING AHEAD TO THE CHAMPIONS LEAGUE, MAY 2016

FOR THE FIRST TIME IN THEIR LIVES, THE PEOPLE CAN WIN THE LEAGUE. IT IS UNBELIEVABLE. HISTORY. AND WE KNOW IT.

ON MAKING HISTORY, APRIL 2016

I TOLD MY PLAYERS: 'IT'S THIS YEAR OR NEVER. IN AN ERA WHEN MONEY COUNTS FOR EVERYTHING, WE GIVE HOPE TO EVERYBODY.'

ON MOTIVATING HIS PLAYERS, FEBRUARY 2016

I'D LIKE TO SAY, 'YES WE CAN!'
BUT I AM NOT BARACK OBAMA!

WHEN ASKED IF LEICESTER COULD PULL OFF THE BIGGEST SHOCK
IN PREMIER LEAGUE HISTORY, FEBRUARY 2016

IF I COULD HAVE IMAGINED THE PERFECT ENDING TO THIS STORY FOR LEICESTER, THIS IS PRECISELY THE WAY I WOULD HAVE IMAGINED IT, WITH BOCELLI SINGING 'VINCERO' IN THE MIDDLE OF THE STADIUM.

ON A FAIRYTALE ENDING, MAY 2016

WE ARE IN THE CHAMPIONS LEAGUE, DILLY-DING, DILLY-DONG. IT'S FANTASTIC, TERRIFIC. WELL DONE TO EVERYBODY, THE OWNERS, THE FANS, THE PLAYERS, THE STAFF, EVERYBODY INVOLVED IN IT.

CLAUDIO EMPLOYING HIS NOW-SIGNATURE EXPRESSION, APRIL 2016

ONCE IN A LIFE IT CAN HAPPEN.
THAT IS FOOTBALL.

APRIL 2016

ON CLAUDIO 9

I AM ALWAYS HAPPY WHEN OUR FANS ARE HAPPY, WHEN OUR PLAYERS ARE HAPPY AND OUR CHAIRMAN IS ON THE MOON.

POSSIBLE FREUDIAN SLIP? APRIL 2004

SEEING THE POLICE BE HAPPY, IT MAKES ME HAPPY!

*CLAUDIO STAYING ON THE RIGHT SIDE OF THE LAW
AT THE TITLE PARADE, MAY 2016*

SIR CLAUDIO? UNBELIEVABLE! HAS SOMEBODY CALLED ME? NO, NOBODY, BUT I LIKE IT! DON'T JOKE, PLEASE!

WHEN ASKED ABOUT PEOPLE CALLING FOR HIM TO BE AWARDED AN HONORARY KNIGHTHOOD, MAY 2016

I'VE MISSED THE PREMIER LEAGUE, I'VE MISSED ENGLISH FOOTBALL. ENGLISH FOOTBALL IS SPECIAL; THE FANS, THE CROWD, THE ATMOSPHERE IS VERY WARM IN EVERY STADIUM. I LOVE THE RESPECT IN ENGLAND.

WELCOME BACK, CLAUDIO, JULY 2015

ONE BEAUTIFUL DAY, A RADIANT DAY, MR ABRAMOVICH INTRODUCED HIMSELF TO ME AND SAID I SHOULD PUT A SHOPPING LIST TOGETHER.

*A POETIC CLAUDIO EXPLAINING HOW HIS ENGLISH
ADVENTURE BEGAN, SEPTEMBER 2003*

HE WAS THE GREATEST AMBASSADOR AND REPRESENTATIVE OF ITALIAN FOOTBALL, SO I LIKE TO REMEMBER HIM IN THESE MOMENTS.

CLAUDIO THINKS OF GIANFRANCO ZOLA IN HIS MOMENTS OF ELATION, MAY 2016

I SAY MY TEAM IS LIKE THE RAF, IT'S FANTASTIC – WHOOSH WHOOSH! I LOVE IT.

AFTER HEARING THAT MARC ALBRIGHTON, JEFF SCHLUPP AND JAMIE VARDY ARE THE PREMIER LEAGUE'S FASTEST PLAYERS, SEPTEMBER 2015

I WAITED SO LONG BUT I AM SO HAPPY. I DON'T KNOW WHAT WILL HAPPEN NEXT SEASON BECAUSE THIS WAS A MAGIC SEASON. AFTER THE LAST MATCH, LET ME GO TO THE SEA AND RECHARGE MY BATTERIES. AND AFTER THAT WE WILL START.

REFLECTING ON A HISTORIC ACHIEVEMENT, MAY 2016

MAMMA MIA

MY ONLY TECHNICAL ADVISER IS MY MOTHER. WHEN I TOLD HER THAT DAMIEN HAD INJURED HIS SHOULDER AGAIN, SHE SAID, 'OH NO!' WHO SHOULD REPLACE HIM? I WILL CALL HER BEFORE THE GAME TO ASK.

*CLAUDIO REVEALING THE SOURCE OF HIS TECHNICAL ADVICE.
HE WAS SACKED SOON AFTERWARDS, MAY 2004*

DAMIEN IS DAMIEN. WHEN I DON'T PUT HIM IN THE SQUAD MY MOTHER, WHO'S 84, ASKS, 'WHY ISN'T DAMIEN PLAYING?' SHE KILLS ME ABOUT IT AND THAT'S TRUE.

CLAUDIO SPILLING THE BEANS ON HIS MUM'S FAVOURITE PLAYER, APRIL 2004

I'D LIKE TO WATCH THE TOTTENHAM MATCH BUT I'M ON A FLIGHT BACK FROM ITALY. MY MOTHER IS 96 YEARS OLD AND I WOULD LIKE TO HAVE A LUNCH WITH HER. I WILL BE THE LAST MAN IN ENGLAND TO KNOW.

WHEN ASKED IF HE'LL BE WATCHING THE CRUCIAL CHELSEA VS. TOTTENHAM GAME ON 2ND MAY, WHICH SEALED LEICESTER'S PREMIER LEAGUE TITLE

ALL THE NEWSPAPERS [IN ITALY] ARE CALLING HIM THE KING OF ENGLAND, JUST IMAGINE THAT.

RENATA RANIERI ON HER SON'S CROWNING GLORY, MAY 2016

MY SON NEEDS TO STAY FIT, SO HE ALMOST NEVER OPTS FOR A 'PRIMO' (THE PLATE OF PASTA THAT TRADITIONALLY KICKS OFF AN ITALIAN MEAL). INSTEAD HE HAS GREEN BEANS OR A SALAD.

RENATA RANIERI ON CLAUDIO'S DIETARY SECRETS, MAY 2016

EVERY TIME THEY ARE ON TELEVISION I MAKE SURE MARIO (CLAUDIO'S DAD, AGED 92) AND I ARE SITTING DOWN TO WATCH THE GAME TOGETHER. I LIKE TO SEE WHAT CLAUDIO HAS BEEN UP TO AND WHO HE HAS PICKED FOR THE TEAM.

RENATA RANIERI ON HER SON'S FAITHFUL FAMILY FOLLOWING, MAY 2016

SHE IS PROUD BUT SHE IS PROUD BECAUSE I AM AN HONEST MAN AND THAT MAKES ME MORE PROUD.

CLAUDIO ON HIS MOTHER'S PRIDE, MAY 2016

HE'S A CALM AND SERIOUS PERSON BUT HE ALSO KNOWS HOW TO JOKE AROUND. HE IS ABLE TO GAIN PEOPLE'S CONFIDENCE.

ALESSANDRO ROJA, CLAUDIO'S SON-IN-LAW

MY TEAM IS MY BABY.
WHEN IT IS READY TO GET OUT OF THE PRAM,
I WILL LEAD IT BY THE HAND.

CLAUDIO'S PATERNALISTIC APPROACH TO MANAGEMENT, 2003

A PIZZA
HIS MIND

I TOLD THEM, IF YOU KEEP A CLEAN SHEET, I'LL BUY PIZZA FOR EVERYBODY. I THINK THEY'RE WAITING FOR ME TO OFFER A HOT DOG TOO!

CLAUDIO'S TASTY INCENTIVE, SEPTEMBER 2015

I PAY! I THINK THEY DESERVE THIS PIZZA AND TODAY WE WILL EAT. IT'S GOOD TO STAY TOGETHER FOR SOMETHING GOOD [OTHER THAN] FOOTBALL. I THINK ALSO THIS COULD HELP TO MAKE A VERY GOOD SPIRIT FOR EACH OTHER. I HOPE THEY ENJOY IT TODAY.

CLAUDIO HONOURS HIS PIZZA PLEDGE, OCTOBER 2015

I PAY FOR PIZZA, YOU PAY FOR THE SAUSAGE. I AM THE SAUSAGEMAN.

CLAUDIO'S NOW-LEGENDARY ANNOUNCEMENT AFTER BEING TOLD A LEICESTER BUTCHER HAD CREATED A SAUSAGE IN HIS HONOUR, MARCH 2016

LUCK IS THE SALT, THE FANS ARE THE TOMATO – WITH NO TOMATO THERE IS NO PIZZA.

THE RECIPE FOR SUCCESS, OCTOBER 2015

CHAMPAGNE AND PIZZA IS GOOD, NOT FANTASTIC, BUT OK.

CLAUDIO ADDED A DOZEN BOTTLES OF CHAMPAGNE (WHILE HONOURING HIS PIZZA PLEDGE)
AFTER THE TEAM KEPT THEIR FIRST CLEAN SHEET, OCTOBER 2015

MY PLAYERS SHOWED GOOD STAMINA AND GOOD VITAMINS.

CLAUDIO'S SECRET FORMULA AFTER CHELSEA BEAT ARSENAL IN THE CHAMPIONS LEAGUE QUARTER FINAL, 2004

SOMETIMES WE SIT AT THE DINNER TABLE AND I AM FRIGHTENED AT HOW MUCH THEY EAT. I'VE NEVER SEEN PLAYERS SO HUNGRY!

ON THE APPETITE OF HIS SQUAD, FEBRUARY 2016

NO PIZZA TONIGHT, OUR CHAIRMAN HAS INVITED US TO DINNER.

FIRST-CLASS TREATMENT FROM THE BOSS, MAY 2016

NOW WE NEED A BIGGER INCENTIVE.
I MIGHT HAVE TO BUY LUNCH OR DINNER NEXT
SEASON... MAYBE LOBSTER. ONLY ONE.

RAISING THE STAKES FOR THE 2016/7 SEASON

CHAMPIONING
CLAUDIO

JOSÉ MOURINHO WAS THE FIRST PERSON TO SEND ME A MESSAGE SAYING, 'WELCOME BACK CLAUDIO'. HE'S A NICE BOY.

JOSÉ MOURINHO PATCHES THINGS UP WITH HIS OLD RIVAL, AUGUST 2015

CONGRATULATIONS BOSS, YOU REALLY HAVE BEEN BRILLIANT. THIS SUCCESS IS RICHLY DESERVED.

ROMA LEGEND FRANCESCO TOTTI AFTER LEICESTER WON THE PREMIER LEAGUE, MAY 2016

CLAUDIO RANIERI? REALLY?

...I SHOULD EXPLAIN THAT THIS TWEET WAS SENT PREMATURELY. MEANT TO SAY 'CLAUDIO RANIERI? REALLY REALLY BRILLIANT!'

GARY LINEKER MAKES A LATE AMENDMENT TO HIS EARLIER NAYSAYING, MAY 2016

I HAD THE CHANCE TO FALL IN LOVE WITH A LOT OF CLUBS, NOW I'M IN LOVE WITH RANIERI'S LEICESTER. JAMIE VARDY? HE'S VERY GOOD, BUT LEICESTER'S REAL PHENOMENON IS RANIERI. INCREDIBLE.

CAMEROON AND EX-INTER MILAN STRIKER SAMUEL ETO'O IS FULL OF PRAISE, APRIL 2016

MIRACLES DON'T EXIST IN FOOTBALL. THEY HAVE HAD A PHENOMENAL SEASON, RANIERI HAS DONE A PHENOMENAL JOB.

ZINEDINE ZIDANE HAILS CLAUDIO'S RENAISSANCE, MAY 2016

IT'S THE GREATEST ACHIEVEMENT IN THE HISTORY OF ENGLISH FOOTBALL, AND IT WAS LED BY AN ITALIAN #INSANE

PATRIOTIC PRAISE FROM MATTEO RENZI, ITALY'S PRIME MINISTER, ON TWITTER, MAY 2016

I WANT TO CONGRATULATE EVERYONE CONNECTED TO @LCFC; PLAYERS, STAFF, OWNERS AND FANS. I LOST MY TITLE TO CLAUDIO RANIERI AND IT IS WITH INCREDIBLE EMOTION THAT I LIVE THIS MAGIC MOMENT IN HIS CAREER.

A MAGNANIMOUS MOURINHO IS GRACIOUS IN DEFEAT, MAY 2016

HUGE CONGRATS TO EVERYONE AT LEICESTER AND PARTICULARLY CLAUDIO RANIERI. A GENTLEMAN WHO CHANGED MY LIFE.

FRANK LAMPARD ON INSTAGRAM, MAY 2016

ALL THE FOOTBALLING WORLD AT THE FEET OF CLAUDIO RANIERI! HOW WONDERFUL! YOU ARE GREAT!

ITALIAN TENNIS STAR ROBERTA VINCI ON TWITTER, MAY 2016

HE'S LEGENDARY. I WOULD LABEL HIM AN EXAMPLE OF HOW ANYONE SHOULD SPUR HIMSELF TO ACHIEVE THE IMPOSSIBLE IF YOU BELIEVE AND ALL WORK TOWARDS THE SAME GOAL.

FORMER JUVENTUS DEFENDER NICOLA LEGROTTAGLIE, MAY 2016

WE HAVE TO PAY HOMAGE TO A GREAT ITALIAN WHO HAS SHOWN THAT YOU MUST ALWAYS BELIEVE.

ITALIAN PRIME MINISTER MATTEO RENZI, MAY 2016

HE IS LIKE YOUR FAVOURITE TEACHER AT SCHOOL.

LEICESTER DEFENDER ROBERT HUTH, MAY 2016

WHAT RANIERI DID THAT WAS SPECIAL WAS TO GIVE A SENSE OF EMPATHY TO HIS TEAM. IF YOU, AS A PERSON, CAN CREATE AN EMPATHETIC SITUATION INSIDE THE CHANGING ROOM, THEN IN THE DIFFICULT MOMENTS YOUR PLAYERS WILL ALWAYS GIVE YOU A LITTLE SOMETHING MORE.

SIMONE PEROTTA, RETIRED ITALIAN INTERNATIONAL MIDFIELDER, APRIL 2016